COOL CATS
Calm Kids

Relaxation and Stress Management for Young People

Written by Mary L. Williams   Illustrated by Dianne O'Quinn Burke

Impact Publishers®
SAN LUIS OBISPO, CALIFORNIA 93406

Library of Congress Cataloging-in-Publication Data

Williams, Mary (Mary L.), 1944-
  Cool cats, calm kids :   relaxation and stress management for young people / Mary Williams : illustrated by Dianne O'Quinn Burke.
      p.   cm.
  Summary : Uses cats and their lifestyles to present techniques to help young people deal with stress.
  ISBN 0-915166-94-1 (softcover : alk. paper)
  1. Stress in children—Juvenile literature.   2. Stress management for children—Juvenile literature,   3. Relaxation—Juvenile literature.   4. Assertiveness in children—Juvenile literature.
[1. Stress management.   2. Stress (Psychology)]   I. Burke, Dianne O'Quinn,   ill.   II. Title.
BF723.S75W55   1996
155.4' 18—dc20   96-2158
                                                       CIP
                                                        AC

Printed in the United States of America on acid-free paper
Published by **Impact** *Publishers*®
POST OFFICE BOX 1094
SAN LUIS OBISPO, CALIFORNIA 93406

COOL CATS, CALM KIDS is dedicated especially to my last three cats:

Jenny, who "sighs" enormously when she receives too much attention,

Smokey, who could not meow but who was Mr. Affection,

Pumpkin, who delivered his meow-meow in a sing-songy manner.

The book is also dedicated to my husband Leo, who tolerates my cats, and to my adult children Mark and Marla, who have learned their mother's love and respect for cats and kids.

— *Mary Williams*

Do cats really have nine lives?
Maybe so...   ...maybe not.
But if they do, it's because they have
NINE SECRETS
for keeping COOL and CALM.
Here are those secrets, never before shared....

CAT SECRET #1

TAKE CATNAPS.

Have you ever watched a cat find a warm place
and curl up for a few minutes' snooze?

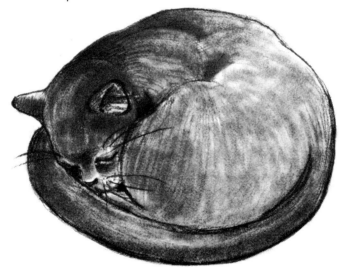

This saves energy for what's really important!
(For a cat, that could just be moving to another warm spot!)

You can CATNAP, too!

First, close your eyes for a few seconds.
Imagine yourself in the warm sunshine...

Then _breathe_ in, clear into your stomach...
and out, slowly... while you tell yourself, *"calm* and *relaxed."*

Keep enjoying the warm sunshine and breathe deeply as you quiet
yourself, letting your worries and tension disappear...

Once you've learned to relax easily,
try catnapping with your eyes open. Then you can catnap anytime
you feel stressed, and no one will know you are calming yourself.
    Your catnap is also the best way to fall asleep!

CAT SECRET #2

STRETCH!

What's the first thing a cat does after a cat nap?
A cat always takes a nice, long, and very slow s t r e t c h.

It gets every little part of the body ready to do what needs to be done (a bath maybe?).

STRETCHING feels <u>sooo</u> good and helps you relax
even when things are going badly...
(like when your mom tells you to clean up your room... when it just
got the way *you* like it!).

CAT SECRET #3

HISS... PUFF UP...

When a cat feels scared or pushed around, she stands up for herself. Her hair standing up means, "I have rights, too, you know."

You don't have to hiss and puff up, but you can ASSERT YOURSELF. Stand tall, look the other person in the eye, and state how you feel or what you want. Oh, and <u>you</u> need to listen to the other person, too, if you want her to listen to you. Then you may be able to find a solution that you <u>both</u> like.

CAT SECRET #4

PLAY AND PLAY SOME MORE!

A cat is always on the look-out for anything that moves ---- it could be a wonderful toy!

It's good to LAUGH and PLAY...
Keep your eyes open for fun, for things
to laugh at...including yourself! And don't
take things too seriously. (Especially when
someone calls you stupid ----
what do they know anyway?)

CAT SECRET #5

HOLD YOUR HEAD HIGH.

No matter what just happened,
a cat will walk away with its head and
      tail held high.

It's a sign that says, "I like myself.
I have this problem handled."
(Even if it is that ridiculous
 dog next door!)

So, HOLD YOUR HEAD HIGH —— especially when you feel left out or embarrassed, like when you fumble for words around that cute kid in class (maybe a cat got your tongue?). Then remind yourself that not *everyone* can like you and that we all make silly

mistakes. Hold your head up and tell yourself, "I won't let this get me down," or, "I'll learn from my mistake."

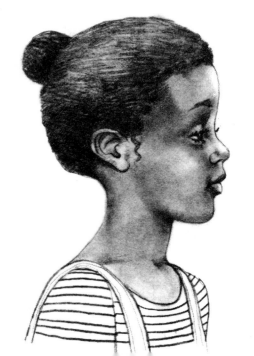

CAT SECRET #6

SPEAK UP.

"Meow... meow...
I want in.
I want out.
I want in."
A cat knows
it never hurts to ask.

So BE HONEST and SPEAK UP!
First, search yourself for how you feel. Sad,
happy, angry or hurt, it is okay to say how
you feel and ask for what you need. Try it —
"Mom, Dad. I'm lonely. Could we do something
together?" It'll work!
(At least sometimes!)

CAT SECRET #7

BE SMART, NOT SNOOTY.

A cat is famous for his INDEPENDENCE.
When he doesn't come when called, or doesn't
sit very long on your
lap, he isn't being
snooty...
He is simply deciding
what is best for himself.

You too can be SMART and INDEPENDENT. Even if a friend pressures you to do something that makes you uncomfortable. It can be hard to say no, and do what you know is best. But when you do, you'll feel better about yourself, knowing you were *smart*!

18

CAT SECRET #8

BE FRIENDLY.

Purr... purr...
Purring is one way a cat gets
what he needs. The purr lets us
know when he is happy with
the way we treat him.

So *smile* and BE FRIENDLY! Let others know when you enjoy how they treat you. A smile and a thank you almost guarantees that someone will try to please you again. This is one way you can contribute to your own happiness.

CAT SECRET #9

HANG IN THERE!

Not only is a cat curious, but she takes risks.
And if she doesn't succeed at something,
she will try, try again.
(Have you ever seen a cat have a
temper tantrum because she didn't
get a bird? Of course not!)

Persistence pays off. This means if you really want something, don't give up! As long as you enjoy what you're doing, keep trying.

Now, *do you think cats have nine lives?*
At least you know they have nine secrets for staying
COOL, CALM, and CONTENTED.
Lets try to remember those secrets:

#1: Quiet yourself, *CATNAP*, tell yourself to be *calm* and *relaxed.*

#2: *S T R E T C H* when you're tense, then let go and become *loose* and *limp*, like a rag doll.

#3: *HISS... PUFF UP...* Stand up for yourself, and work out a fair solution.

#4: *PLAY* and *have fun.* Don't take things too seriously.

#5: *HOLD YOUR HEAD HIGH* and *talk positively* to yourself: "Be patient. I can do this if I stay calm and relaxed. I like myself, even if I'm not perfect. (Nobody is!)"

#6: *SPEAK UP...* Ask yourself, "How do I feel?" *Be honest!* And SPEAK UP —– your feelings are important!

#7: Remember, being *independent* is SMART, NOT SNOOTY.

#8: Purr... purr! *BE FRIENDLY* and *smile!*

#9: *HANG IN THERE!* If at first you don't succeed, *try, try again.*

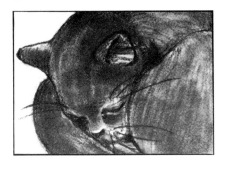

#1 CATNAP

#4 PLAY

#2 STRETCH

#3 HISS

#5 HOLD HEAD
(and tail) HIGH

#9 HANG
IN THERE

#6 SPEAK UP

#8 BE
FRIENDLY

#7 BE SMART

AN ADULT "PURR-SPECTIVE": A BRIEF GUIDE TO STRESS MANAGEMENT

Imagine juggling five balls with no practice, before a crowd. The balls fall, your cheeks flush, your chest pounds, you think, "You idiot!" Children today need our help "juggling" their many stressors.

<u>**Signs and Symptoms of Stress**</u> — If your child often has any of the following, she may be stressed:
- Headaches
- Stomach problems
- Sleeping problems
- Irritability
- Teeth grinding
- Fears
- Inability to cope, tearful
- Feelings of rejection
- Anxiety, nervousness
- Depression, withdrawal
- Cold hands
- Muscular pains

<u>**Stress-Busting Strategies — the Parental Role**</u>
- Try not to over-extend your child with activities. Children need time to daydream!
- Remember, perfection is not the goal in life. Demonstrate the ability to laugh at yourself.
- Practice these stress-reducing skills with your child: 1) stand and stretch, bend over — go limp, 2) smooth your brow, loosen your jaw, roll your head around, 3) shrug your shoulders, give massages.
- Be alert for self put-downs: "I can't...," "No one likes me...," "I'm dumb," Acknowledge your child's feeling: "You're discouraged, aren't you?" Then validate the feeling: "It's hard when you're unsure of yourself." Reflect the feelings until they seem to evaporate. Encourage with a positive self-statement: "When I slow down and relax, I can do this." "Not everybody can like me all the time, but I like myself." Boosting self-esteem with self-talk is the quintessence of stress management.

Deep Breathing

Most of us are unaware that we breathe too fast and/or hold our breath for periods of time. The foundation of stress management is deep breathing. Slow, deep breathing promotes relaxation. First, become aware of your breathing pattern, then practice breathing exercises to enable yourself (or your child) to react to stress appropriately.

<u>Awareness</u> — Have your child place one hand on the chest and one on the stomach and then ask: "How does your breathing feel (relaxed or stiff)?" "Does your chest or stomach move when you breathe?" Holding one's breath, or stiff "chest" breathing indicates the need for more relaxed breathing.

<u>Breathing Exercises</u> — Practice each separately and then together. Practice many times a day: as you awaken or fall asleep, before a test, when in conflict with someone.
    1. *Slow breathing* — Breathe in slowly, counting one, two, three, four, hold; breathe out slowly, counting one, two, three, four; hold, repeat.
    2. *Deeper breathing* — Place one hand on the chest, the other on the abdomen. Imagine a balloon in your abdomen blowing up as you breathe in — your hand on the abdomen rises; the balloon deflates as you breathe out— your hand falls. The hand on the chest stays fairly constant.
    3. *Calm and relaxed*— When breathing in, tell yourself, "I am calm"; when breathing out, tell yourself, "I am relaxed."

Remember, deep, slow breathing is the fastest way to calm yourself!

MORE RESOURCES FOR STRESS MANAGEMENT

Breathe Away Distress (audio), Sylvia Lincoln, Stress Mastery Biofeedback Lab, 614 Traver Trail, Glenwood Springs, CO 81601.

How To Talk So Your Kids Will Listen (audio), Adele Faber and Elaine Maglish, Simon and Schuster, 1230 Ave. of the Americas, New York, NY 10020.

I Am Precious (audio), and *My Precious Child* (pb), Mary L. Williams, Box 1524, Glenwood Springs, CO 81602.

The Mouse, The Monster & Me (pb), Pat Palmer, Ed.D., Impact Publishers, Inc., PO Box 1094, San Luis Obispo, CA 93406.

The Relaxation and Stress Reduction Workbook (pb), Martha Davis, Elizabeth Robbins Eshelman, Matthew McKay, New Harbinger Publ., Inc., 5674 Shattuck Ave., Oakland, CA 94609.

Taming Your Dragons (audio/pb), Martha Belknapp, 1170 Dixon Rd./Gold Hill, Boulder, CO 80302.

Tense-Slow-Relax (audio), Biofeedback Systems, 2736 47th St., Boulder, Co 80301.

MORE BOOKS BY MARY WILLIAMS

(All published by Health Communications, Inc., Deerfield Beach, FL): *My Precious Child*, 1991; *God's Precious Girl*, 1992, *God's Precious Boy*, 1992; *Let's Celebrate Our Differences*, 1994.

MORE LITTLE IMP® BOOKS

LIKING MYSELF
Pat Palmer, Ed.D.
$7.95 80 pages
A friendly introduction to feelings, self-esteem and assertiveness for youngsters 5-9.

"I WISH I COULD HOLD YOUR HAND": A Child's Guide to Grief and Loss
Pat Palmer, Ed.D.
$7.95 32 pages
A warm and comforting guide to understanding and working through the pain of loss.

THE MOUSE, THE MONSTER & ME
Pat Palmer, Ed.D.
$6.95 80 pages
Children who learn to be assertive feel good about themselves. Ages 8 & up.

TEEN ESTEEM: A Self-Direction Manual for Young Adults
Pat Palmer, Ed.D. with M.A. Froehner
$7.95 128 pages
Helps teens handle peer pressure, substance abuse, other choices and challenges.

Ask your local bookseller, or write for our free catalog. Prices effective April 1996 and subject to change without notice.

Impact 🐌 Publishers®
POST OFFICE BOX 1094
SAN LUIS OBISPO, CALIFORNIA 93406